ENERGY

John Woodruff

Photography by
Chris Fairclough

RSVP®

RAINTREE
STECK-VAUGHN
PUBLISHERS
The Steck-Vaughn Company

Austin, Texas

Published by Raintree Steck-Vaughn Publishers,
an imprint of Steck-Vaughn Company.

Library of Congress Cataloging-in-Publication Data
Woodruff, John.
Energy / John Woodruff.
     p.   cm.—(Science Projects)
     Includes bibliographical references and index.
     Summary: Explains the concept of energy through
     experiments which can be performed at home.
     ISBN 0-8172-4961-3
     1. Force and energy—Juvenile literature.
     [1. Force and energy—Experiments. 2. Experiments.]
     I. Fairclough, Chris, ill. II. Title
     III. Series: Science projects.
     QC73.4.W67   1998
     531'.6—dc21   97-33986

Printed in Italy. Bound in the United States.
1 2 3 4 5 6 7 8 9 0 02 01 00 99 98

Picture acknowledgments:
The publishers would like to thank the following for
permission to reproduce their pictures:
Eurostar: p38; **NASA:** p4; **Robert Harding Picture
Library:** pages 16 (R. Maisonneuve Publiphoto), 19
(Bill Ross), 28, 44 (Tony Gervis); **Tony Stone Images:**
pages 8 (Glyn Kirk), 20 (A & L Sinibaldi), 26 (Ed
Pritchard), 28 (Rosemary Weller), 30 (Mark A. Leman),
32 (A & L Sinibaldi), 34 (Peter/Stef Lamberti), 40 (Nadia
Mackenzie); **Science Photo Library:** 10 (Oscar
Burrie/Latin Stock), 14 (Alfred Pasieha), 22 (Martin
Dohrn), 31 (Peter Menzel), 36 (Jean-Loup Charmet),
42 (James-King Holmes, cover (Julian Balm).
Illustrations: Mick Gillah, Julian Baker cover and pages
5, 11, 25 and 44

CONTENTS

WHAT IS ENERGY?

Wherever there is movement, whenever anything is changing in some way, energy is involved. We often say that people who feel tired don't have much energy, or that people who do strenuous work or exercise use up a lot of energy. All living things require energy to keep them going. All devices and machines, from a watch powered by a tiny battery to the space shuttle burning rocket fuel as it blasts into orbit, use energy too.

Energy is what makes things work. Anything that is doing work, whether it is alive or a machine, is changing one type of energy into another. When you run, your body converts the chemical energy from food into the energy of your movement. Some is converted into heat, another form of energy, for you will feel hotter. Gas stoves turn the chemical energy in gas into heat for cooking. A television set turns electrical energy into sound and light—two more forms of energy.

In the modern world we get our energy from many sources. The electricity we use, for example, may come from the chemical energy in coal, the energy of flowing rivers, or directly from the sun. Most forms of energy we use can be traced back to the sun, but nuclear energy comes from breaking apart the atoms from which everything is made.

The launch of a space shuttle. A rocket needs to use a huge amount of fuel to produce enough energy to overcome the pull of the earth's gravity.

DID YOU KNOW?

The word "energy" in its modern scientific sense was first used in the early 1800s by the English doctor Thomas Young to describe the energy of moving objects.

AN ENERGY SURVEY

This is a survey of different types of energy in action, like heat and light. You will be looking at different energy sources later in the book.

MATERIALS
• a notebook and pencil

1. First, decide where you are going to carry out your survey. You could pick a room in your house or your classroom.

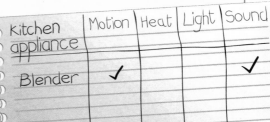

Kitchen appliance	Motion	Heat	Light	Sound
Blender	✓			✓

2. Decide how to record your findings. You could make a list in the kitchen, as above. What types of energy are produced? Which type occurs most often? Does any appliance produce all the types of energy you have listed? How about a microwave?

3. Think about how different types of energy are used at different times of the day or year. How is energy used differently at night or in another season?

4. Think of some other places where you could do an energy survey. How about trying a supermarket or a railroad station?

WAVES AND VIBRATIONS

Waves are an important way in which energy is transferred from one place to another. If you flip one end of a hose that is stretched out, or a long piece of string, you will see a wave travel toward the other end. This wave is transferring energy of motion.

When something vibrates—when it shakes back and forth rapidly—it makes things next to it vibrate as well. As these things vibrate, in turn they cause others next to them to vibrate, setting up a chain of vibrations. That is how sound reaches our ears.

A sound wave travels through the air when molecules (particles) in the air make one another vibrate.

Although waves transfer energy from one place to another, what the waves pass through remains in the same place. Each part of the hose or string moves up and down as the wave travels along it. However, the hose or string itself does not move either toward or away from you. In the same way, the air through which a sound wave travels doesn't move toward you.

TRANSFERRING ENERGY

1. Make two loops in the long length of string about 10 in. (25 cm) from each end, and tie the ends to the broom handle.

MATERIALS

- a broom handle
- three lengths of string, one 3 ft. (1 m) long and two 20 in. (50 cm) long
- two large nuts

2. Tie a nut to the end of each shorter string to make two pendulums, and tie the pendulums to the loops.

3. Lay the broom handle between two supports of the same height so that it is horizontal. Wait until the weights have stopped moving.

4. Hold one weight steady while you set the other swinging. Take care not to let it swing by more than 4 in. (10 cm). Swings greater than this tend to become irregular and jerky.

5. Now let go of the other weight. Keep watching. What happens and why?

Most of the energy we use on Earth comes from the sun's light and heat, which reach us in the form of electromagnetic radiation. This radiation travels as invisible waves that move through space at the speed of 186,000 mi. (300,000 km) every second. Radio waves are also of this type.

TRANSFERRING MORE ENERGY

1. With a ruler, draw two lines along the strip of cardboard. Fold up the edges along these lines to make a track about 1 in. (2.5 cm) wide. Slit opposite edges of your track about 4 in. (10 cm) from one end so you can bend the track at this point to make a ramp. Use the wooden block to raise the ramp.

2. Place all the ball bearings but one on the level part of the track so that they are just touching. Release the remaining ball bearing down the ramp. The ball bearing at the far end should move: the other ball bearings have transferred the moving one's energy along the "chain."

3. What happens if you release two or more ball bearings together down the ramp?

MATERIALS
- several ball bearings of the same size
- a strip of cardboard 20–30 in. (50–75 cm) long and 2.5 in. (6 cm) wide
- a wooden block 1.25 in. (3 cm) high
- a ruler
- scissors

MAKING WATER WAVES

1. Half fill a bowl with water and place a cork near the middle of the bowl.

2. When the water is still, disturb the surface of the water with your finger. What happens? If you shine the flashlight onto the water you will see the effect more clearly.

MATERIALS
- a bowl of water
- a cork
- a flashlight

FORMS OF ENERGY

All things that move have what is called kinetic energy. The faster something moves, the more kinetic energy it has. An object's kinetic energy also depends on its mass (how heavy it is): a heavier object will have more kinetic energy than a lighter one moving at the same speed. A lumbering tortoise has more kinetic energy than a

A ski jumper converts the potential energy he has gained by climbing to the top of the jump into kinetic energy as he skis downhill.

MEASURE KINETIC ENERGY

MATERIALS

- a piece of board about 3 ft. (91 cm) long
- wooden blocks or books as props
- a toy car or truck
- a tape measure
- a notebook and pencil

Do this experiment in a room with a smooth floor, not in one with a carpet.

1. Make a ramp by propping up one end of the board. Make the slope fairly gentle at first, raising one end by about 4 in. (10 cm). Measure and record the height. Draw a starting line near the top of the slope.

2. Place the car in front of the starting line and release it down the slope.

3. Record how far the car has traveled by measuring from the starting line to the back of the car.

4. Repeat steps **2** and **3** twice and find the average of the three measurements.

changes into kinetic energy as his speed increases. A swinging pendulum converts potential energy into kinetic energy and back again with every swing. This type of potential energy is called gravitational potential energy because the skier and the pendulum had to overcome the pull of the earth's gravity in moving to a higher position. Gravitational potential energy depends on an object's mass, and also on how high the object has been lifted.

scampering mouse, despite the fact that the mouse moves more quickly, because the tortoise is so much heavier.

An object has potential energy if it has energy stored in it. It can have potential energy simply by being in a certain position. A ski jumper gains potential energy by climbing to the top of a ski slope. As the skier starts to ski downhill, this potential energy

5. Now raise the end of the ramp to about 8 in. (20 cm) and repeat steps **2** to **4**.

6. Continue raising the ramp and repeating steps **2** to **4**. Be careful not to make the ramp too steep as the car will "crash-land" instead of running across the floor.

7. What can you tell from your results? Do you think that using a heavier car would make any difference?

CONVERTING ENERGY

We have seen how potential energy can be converted into kinetic energy. Other examples of energy conversion are all around us. In the natural world, animals store chemical energy from food and convert it in their muscles and tissues to kinetic energy in order to function and move around. In our homes, electrical energy is converted into heat, light, sound, and kinetic energy in various household appliances.

A series of energy changes can be thought of as an "energy chain." When you light a candle with a match, you convert chemical energy you obtained from food into muscular ("mechanical") energy to strike the match. The chemical energy in the match head changes into heat (plus some light) that is transferred to the candle. Then the chemical energy in the candle wax is converted into light (plus some heat).

Energy can't be created out of nothing, and it can't be destroyed. Energy can only be converted from one form to another. Scientists call this the law of conservation of energy. Even when it seems that energy has been lost somewhere, it has only been converted into another form.

All machines appear to "lose" some energy by converting energy into a form that isn't useful. A car engine, for example, doesn't convert all the chemical energy of its fuel into kinetic energy: some ends up as heat and

A match head has chemical energy stored in it. When the match is lit, the chemical energy is converted into heat and light.

sound. Sometimes it isn't obvious where the energy goes. What happens to the kinetic energy of a boulder pushed over a cliff when it hits the ground? Some will be converted into sound and some will be transferred as heat to the earth as happens with most collisions. The earth will also move a little, but because it is so massive compared with the boulder, the amount the earth moves is so small that it can't be measured.

ENERGY CHAINS AT HOME

MATERIALS

• a notebook and pencil

1. Do this survey in your kitchen. You will probably find plenty of energy chains that start with electricity, but you may have an energy chain that starts with gas.

2. Record your findings by dividing up the chains according to the first form of energy in the chain. For each chain, think about how energy is being transformed into less useful forms as well as useful ones. What types of less useful energy are formed the most often?

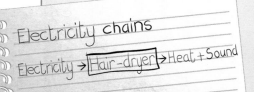

Electricity chains

Electricity → Hair-dryer → Heat + Sound

3. Ask some friends to do their own surveys and compare everyone's results.

CONSERVATION OF ENERGY

MATERIALS

• two lengths of string, one about 4 in. (10 cm) long, the other 5 ft. (1.5 m) long
• an empty thread spool
• an empty yogurt container
• modeling clay & scissors

1. Make two holes in the yogurt container opposite each other below the rim.

2. Press some modeling clay into the base of the pot. Thread one end of the short length of string through one hole and tie the string securely. Thread the other end through the opposite hole and again tie securely.

3. Tie the long length of string to the center of your string handle.

WARNING!

• Do this experiment outdoors in a clear area.

Thread the other end of the string through the hole in the center of the spool.

4. Hold the free end of the string in one hand and the spool over your head with the other hand. Now swing the container in a large circle. Take note of how fast it goes around.

5. Keeping the spool at the same height, pull the free end of the string down so that the container travels in a smaller circle. What happens, and why?

STORING ENERGY

We need to store energy so that we can make use of it whenever we need to. Such stored energy is called potential energy. Most energy, such as kinetic energy or light, is stored as potential energy. This is because it is either difficult or impossible to store directly. Many small common devices, such as flashlights or razors, are powered by batteries in which stored chemical energy is converted into electrical energy.

Domestic fuels are a chemical means of storing energy. Oil, kerosene, and gas are used for heating and cooking and gasoline and diesel fuel for powering vehicles. Coal, wood, and peat are fossil fuels and are more traditional forms of natural stored chemical energy.

MAKE A CRAWLER

1. Make a wax "washer" by cutting about .5 in. (1 cm) from the flat end of the candle. Use the screwdriver to enlarge the hole where the wick passed through. Cut a shallow groove across one face of the "washer."

2. Push the rubber band through the hole in the washer so that one end just pokes through. Now push the long match through the loop.

MATERIALS
- an empty thread spool
- a strong rubber band, about half as long again as the spool
- a long match and a short match
- a candle
- a modeling knife
- a screwdriver
- masking or packing tape

3. Pass the other end of the rubber band through the hole in the spool. Pull it tight so that the long match sits in the groove in the washer.

WARNING!
- Ask an adult to cut the candle for you.

4. Push the short match through the second loop and tape it firmly to the spool. Store energy in the crawler by turning the long match to twist the rubber band.

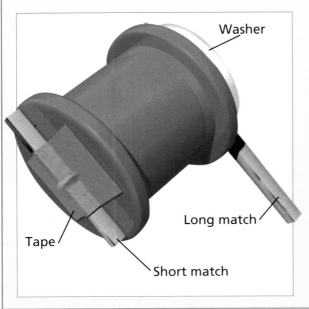

Washer

Long match

Tape

Short match

5. When you put the crawler down and let go of the long match, it will start to crawl.

6. Devise some tests for your crawler. You could see how far the crawler travels with different rubber bands and different numbers of twists. Try the crawler up and down a ramp. You can probably predict how the results will differ, but can you say why?

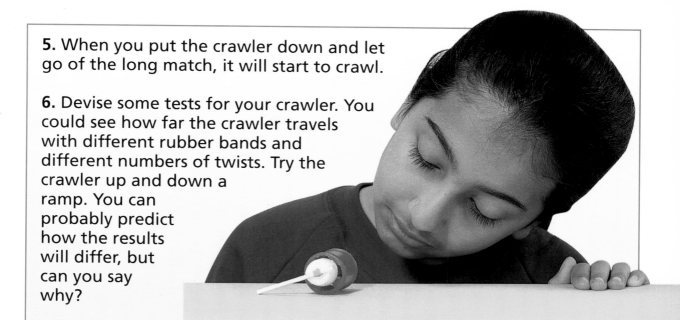

A RETURNING CRAWLER

1. Use the hammer and nail to make two holes in the lid and two holes in the base of the can.

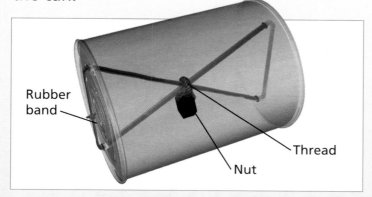

Rubber band

Thread

Nut

MATERIALS

- an empty can with a removable lid
- a length of strong round elastic or a cut rubber band
- a short length of strong thread
- a heavy nut
- a hammer
- a large nail

WARNING!

- Be careful when piercing the holes in the can.

2. Thread the rubber band through the holes in the base and cross the ends inside the can. Next thread the ends through the holes in the lid. Tie them securely as shown in the diagram.

3. Use the thread to tie the nut tightly to the elastic where the two strands cross inside the can. Replace the lid on the can.

4. Gently roll the can away from you, not too fast. What happens? Can you explain why?

HEAT AND TEMPERATURE

Heat, as we have seen, is a form of energy. We measure how hot something is by its temperature. But the temperature of an object does not tell us how much heat energy it contains. Just as the slow-moving tortoise has more kinetic energy than a fast-moving mouse (see pages 8–9), a saucepan of warm water has more heat energy than a red-hot needle.

Heat energy will transfer from a hot body to a cooler one placed next to it, but never the other way around. An ice cube chills a drink because heat energy is transferred from the drink to the ice cube.

Atoms and molecules—the particles of which everything is made—are in constant vibration, but they are so small that this motion is detectable only

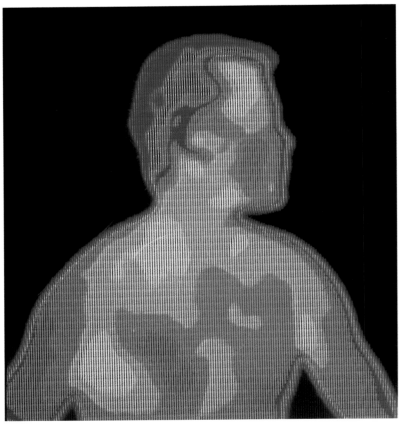

This color thermograph maps the spread of heat over a man's head and upper body. The blue color shows the coolest parts, moving through green, pink, red, and orange to yellow for the hottest area.

through microscopes. When an object is heated, its atoms and molecules gain energy and move more quickly. It is this "atomic speed" that temperature measures. When a solid object is heated, its atoms vibrate more and it expands. If it could be cooled to the lowest possible temperature, known as absolute zero, which is -459.4° F (-273° C), its atoms would have no kinetic energy at all.

DID YOU KNOW?

Large metal structures can expand a lot on hot days. The main span of a metal bridge has gaps at each end, covered by metal plates, and rests on rollers so that its expansion will not cause the bridge to buckle.

DEMONSTRATING EXPANSION

1. Set the two blocks as far apart as the length of pipe.

2. Lay the darning needle on one of these blocks so that one end sticks out over the edge of the block.

3. Lay the length of pipe across the two blocks so that it rests across the darning needle at one end.

4. Cut out a small disk of cardboard and make a gauge by drawing an arrow on it. Push the disk onto the end of the darning needle. Rest the third block on the pipe at the other end.

5. Light the candle and carefully heat the length of pipe at a point midway between the blocks. Keep an eye on your gauge. What happens and why?

6. If you can find suitable lengths of different metals, you can repeat the test and compare how much they expand. What extra step would you take to make sure that these additional tests were fair?

CONDUCTION

Heat energy is transferred in three different ways: by conduction, convection, or radiation. Conduction is how heat energy is transferred through solid objects, like the copper pipe in the expansion test on page 15.

The most efficient conductors of heat are metals, and the best of those are silver and copper. Non-metals, such as wood or plastic, conduct heat poorly. The least conductive of them are used as insulators to prevent heat from escaping. Good conductors feel cold when you touch them, because they quickly conduct heat away from your hand. Poor conductors feel warm to the touch.

A welder at work. Metals can be welded because they conduct heat well, so the parts to be joined melt and bond quickly.

Saucepans are made of metal so that heat energy can be transferred through them rapidly to cook the food inside. Good-quality saucepans often have copper bottoms. The handles of saucepans may be made of wood or plastic so that you can pick them up without burning your hand.

DID YOU KNOW?

In 1815 Humphry Davy invented a lamp that could be used safely in mine tunnels, where there are often explosive gases. The lamp's flame was surrounded by a wire gauze that conducted the heat away from the flame and kept it from igniting the gases outside the gauze.

Conduction does not work by moving hot material from one place to another. Instead, the atoms of the material pass on vibrations to each other, rather like the way sound waves travel (see pages 24–25). In metals, tiny particles called electrons are free to move around and carry additional heat energy from hot to cool regions. This makes metals good heat conductors.

INVESTIGATING CONDUCTION

1. Use the pliers to bend the wire into a shape that will sit over the rim of the mug, as shown in the diagram.

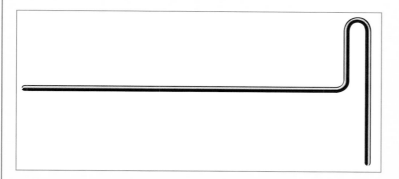

2. Hang the wire over the rim of the mug.

3. Hold the ruler against the wire. Stick pins to the wire a little over 1 in. (2.5 cm) apart by smearing the pinheads with a little petroleum jelly.

4. With your watch, notebook, and pencil ready, ask an adult to fill the mug with boiling water. As heat is conducted along the wire, the petroleum jelly will melt and the pins will fall.

5. Note the time at which the first pin falls and the times at which the other pins fall. What can you tell from your results?

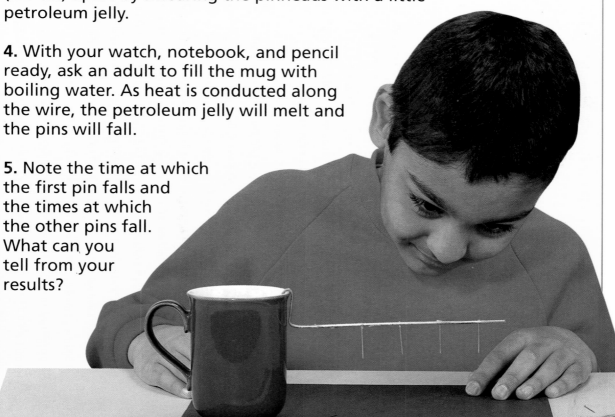

CONVECTION

Convection is the way in which heat energy is transferred through liquids and gases. The heat energy that passes into the liquid or gas causes movement, and convection currents are set up.

When water in a kettle is heated, it expands. This makes it less dense and lighter, and so it rises. This makes way for colder water to move in and take its place. That cold water in turn heats up and rises. In this way, convection currents are set up in which water circulates from the bottom to the top of the kettle and back again, getting hotter each time until the water boils.

Similar convection currents transfer heat energy in gases. Warm air rising over a bonfire carries with it particles of ash, seen as smoke, and cold air is drawn into the fire, keeping it burning. The heat energy is converted into kinetic energy.

CONVECTION IN A LIQUID

MATERIALS
- a small aquarium tank
- a small glass jar
- food coloring or ink
- a large piece of white cardboard or poster board
- aluminum foil
- scissors
- thread
- needle

1. Make a lid for your jar by cutting out a circle of aluminum foil slightly larger than the opening of the jar. Tie as large a knot as you can in the thread and with the needle pull the thread through the center of your foil lid.

2. Fill the aquarium with cold water and place the white cardboard behind it.

3. Put a level teaspoon of food coloring in the small jar and fill it with moderately hot water. Secure the foil lid as tightly as you can around the top and neck of the jar.

4. Gently lower the jar into the aquarium. Wait while the water settles again.

5. Taking care to disturb the water as little as possible, pull the thread to lift the foil and watch what happens.

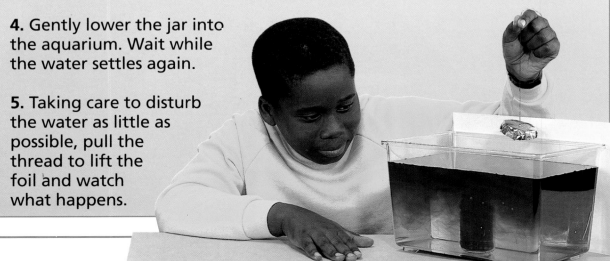

Like hawks and other birds with large wings, glider pilots and hang-gliders gain height when they fly by using columns of warm air, called "thermals," which rise from the ground on hot days. The birds and gliders are making use of a change of heat energy into gravitational potential energy.

CONVECTION IN A GAS

1. Make a fan by cutting a circle 2.5 in. (6 cm) in diameter out of the base of the foil container. Make eight cuts as shown in the diagram.

2. Give each blade a slight twist. Make a small dent in the center of the fan. Be careful not to make a hole.

Cut

3. Push the sharp end of the darning needle into the candle, about .5 in. (1 cm) from the wick. Be sure that the darning needle is vertical.

4. Balance the fan on the top of the needle. Light the candle. The rising convection current should make the fan spin around. If it doesn't turn the first time, blow out the candle, and adjust the "pitch" of the fan's blades.

MATERIALS

- a large candle with a flat top
- a darning needle
- a foil food container
- scissors
- a box of safety matches

WARNING!

- Ask an adult to light the candle for you.

RADIATION

Another way that heat energy is transferred through gases is by radiation. Radiation is also the only way in which heat energy can be transferred through a vacuum. Heat energy from the sun reaches us by radiation, first through the vacuum of space and then through the earth's atmosphere.

Astronomers have learned much about the universe by studying radio waves from far off in space. The waves are collected by radio "telescopes" —giant dish-shaped antennas.

INVESTIGATING RADIANT HEAT

1. Hammer the first nail through the center of the board 4 in. (10 cm) from one end. Hammer the second nail 4 in. (10 cm) away from the first nail. Tap the two dowel lengths onto the nails.

2. Tape the two thermometers onto the two dowel lengths at the same height.

3. Position the lamp next to the board so that it is 4 in. (10 cm) away from the nearest thermometer. Wait about 10 minutes for the thermometers to adjust to the temperature of their surroundings and then switch on the lamp.

4. Look to see which thermometer shows the highest rise in temperature. Record your finding.

MATERIALS

- a piece of board at least 12 in. (30 cm) long
- two lengths of dowel 12 in. (30 cm) long
- a tape measure
- a hammer
- two small nails slightly longer than the thickness of the board
- a powerful desk lamp
- two thermometers
- masking tape
- a notebook and pencil

Heat transferred by radiation—known as radiant heat—is a form of electromagnetic wave called "infrared." Unlike conduction and convection, radiant heat is not carried by particles passing on energy from one to another, or moving from one place to another. All forms of electromagnetic radiation transfer energy. Other examples are radio waves used for broadcasting, and microwaves used in cooking.

Everything radiates heat energy in the form of infrared waves. Objects at higher temperatures radiate more heat energy. In a central-heating system, heat from circulating water is conducted through metal radiators, then radiated into the room. If you turn up the system's main thermostat, the water gets hotter and the radiators radiate more heat energy.

Some burglar alarms are designed to pick up the heat radiated from an intruder's body. Special detectors used by emergency services to find people trapped in the rubble of a collapsed building work the same way. The remote-control handsets that control or "communicate" with television sets and stereo systems also use infrared radiation.

5. Continue to take readings at regular intervals and record the results after each reading. How might you best present your results?

6. Find more thermometers and extend your wooden frame with more lengths of dowel.

LIGHT AS ENERGY

Light is yet another form of electromagnetic radiation and is also a way of transferring energy from one place to another. Sunlight is also the main source of energy for all plant life. Plants have evolved a way of using the light energy from the sun to manufacture food in their leaves. They take carbon dioxide from the air and water from the soil and use sunlight to turn it into oxygen and substances called carbohydrates, which they use as food. Humans and all animals need oxygen. When we breathe in, we extract oxygen from the air and breathe out carbon dioxide. In this way plants and animals produce gases that are necessary to one another. In turn, many animals rely on plants as a major source of energy in the form of food.

Chlorophyll is a green pigment in leaves that enables a plant to absorb sunlight. The light is converted into energy. Plants need this energy to turn carbon dioxide and water into food. This process is known as photosynthesis.

If plants are deprived of sunlight, they wither and die. Look at the grass under an object that has been left on a lawn for a few days and you will find that it has turned yellow. That is because it has been cut off from its supply of energy.

DID YOU KNOW?

A beam of light "pushes" slightly against the surface upon which it shines. This radiation pressure, as it is called, usually has very little effect. But some space engineers have suggested that future interplanetary spacecraft could be powered by radiation pressure "blowing" giant sails a mile or more in diameter.

PHOTOSYNTHESIS

It is important to make sure that the two sets of cress seeds used in this experiment are treated exactly the same way, except that one of them will be kept in the dark.

1. Stand the seed trays on the baking tray. Line both of the seed trays with absorbent cotton. Use the same amount of cotton for each tray.

2. Fill the measuring cup with water, and soak the cotton in each tray. Make sure that each is given the same amount of water. There should be very little excess water in the trays—it should all be absorbed by the cotton.

3. Open one packet of cress seeds and sprinkle the seeds as evenly as you can over the cotton. Then do the same for the other tray. Read the instructions on the packet: you may have to keep both trays covered for a few days to allow the seeds to germinate.

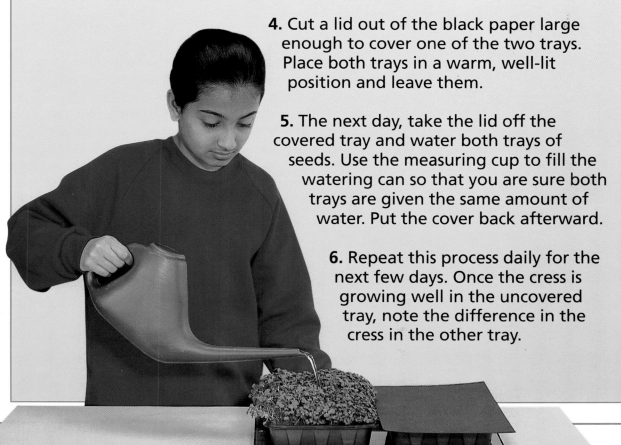

4. Cut a lid out of the black paper large enough to cover one of the two trays. Place both trays in a warm, well-lit position and leave them.

5. The next day, take the lid off the covered tray and water both trays of seeds. Use the measuring cup to fill the watering can so that you are sure both trays are given the same amount of water. Put the cover back afterward.

6. Repeat this process daily for the next few days. Once the cress is growing well in the uncovered tray, note the difference in the cress in the other tray.

MATERIALS
● two seed trays
● a roll of absorbent cotton
● a measuring cup
● two packets of cress seeds
● a piece of black paper or cardboard
● a large metal baking tray
● a small watering can

SOUND AS ENERGY

As we saw on page 6, sound is a form of energy that travels as waves. The waves can be started by a vibration from, for example, a guitar string, a loudspeaker cone, a washing machine, or a pneumatic drill, which makes molecules of air next to it vibrate. They, in turn, make neighboring molecules vibrate, and so on until the molecules of air next to your eardrum vibrate. An energy change then takes place in the middle ear, as vibrations pass through three tiny bones called the hammer, the anvil, and the stirrup. These vibrations then pass into the inner ear and through the fluid in a bony tube called the cochlea. Nerve cells in the cochlea change the vibrations in the liquid into electrical signals that are sent to your brain.

Sound energy travels through air at about 1,080 ft. (330 m) per second. This is much slower than the speed of light.

DID YOU KNOW?

In 1705 a scientist named Francis Hauksbee demonstrated that sound cannot travel through a vacuum. He experimented by placing a clock inside a vacuum chamber. With no air in the chamber, the ticking of the clock could not be heard.

A SIMPLE TELEPHONE

1. Using the pencil, make a small hole in the bottom of the two polystyrene cups.

2. Thread one end of the string through the hole in one of the cups and tie it to a match. Now do the same with the other cup.

MATERIALS

- two identical polystyrene cups
- a 40–50-ft. (12–15-m) length of string
- scissors
- two used matches
- a notebook and pencil
- a sponge
- a bowl of water

3. You have made your telephone. When you speak into one cup, your friend listens to the other cup. You will both have to keep the string between the cups taut so that the matches are kept in contact with the bottoms of the cups.

4. Make two copies of a short message and give a copy to a friend, who will be the recorder.

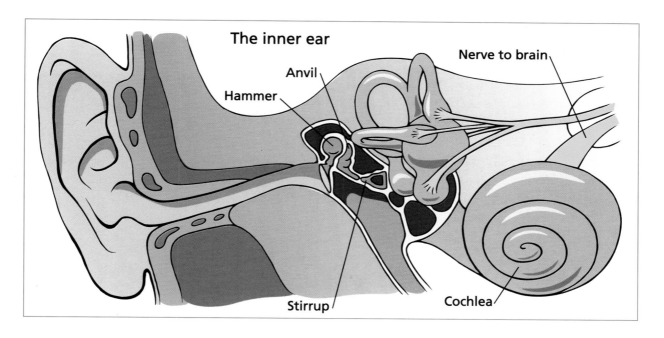

The inner ear

Anvil

Hammer

Nerve to brain

Stirrup

Cochlea

But when sound energy is transferred through solids and liquids, it travels much faster. It travels at about 3,100 mi. (5,000 km) per second through most metals, and at 4,600 ft. (1,400 m) per second through water.

5. Ask a second friend to be the listener. The listener should not have seen the message and should listen at one end of the telephone while you read the message into the other end just once. The listener then repeats the message to the recorder, who counts each correct word and totals a score.

6. Wet the sponge and dampen the entire length of the string between the two cups.

7. Repeat step **5** while the string is still wet. Is the score any higher?

8. You could try the activity again using a different friend as the listener. You could also try a longer length of string.

CHEMICAL ENERGY

All matter is made up of very tiny particles called atoms. In most substances, atoms are joined together to make molecules. Each molecule has a certain energy. When there is a chemical reaction between two substances, the atoms in their molecules are rearranged to make different molecules. If the new molecules have less energy than the old ones, the chemical reaction releases energy. This is where chemical energy comes from.

Chemical energy is usually obtained from combustion, that is, from burning certain substances. Such substances are known as fuels. Particularly important

MAKE A CHEMICAL VOLCANO

1. Using the funnel, half fill one of the bottles with the vinegar. Now add a teaspoonful of red food coloring.

2. Put one or two tablespoons of baking soda into the second bottle.

3. Stand the second bottle on the tray and pile sand around it to make the volcano. Coat the parts of the bottle sticking up through the sand with the glue and pile up more sand around it. Make sure you keep the top clear.

4. Using the funnel, pour in some of the colored vinegar solution from the other bottle. Remove the funnel quickly and watch the volcano erupt.

MATERIALS
- an old tin tray, about 10 in. x 14 in. (25 cm x 35 cm)
- two 12 oz. (330 ml) plastic bottles
- a funnel
- sand
- red food coloring
- baking soda
- white vinegar
- a teaspoon and a tablespoon
- glue
- a long, straight stick

WARNING!
- Do not experiment with ingredients other than those listed here.

Fireworks store chemical energy that is converted into kinetic energy and sound and light energy, as well as some heat energy.

sources of chemical energy are fossil fuels. Most road vehicles are powered by an internal combustion engine, which burns gasoline or diesel fuel and converts chemical energy into kinetic energy. Food is also a form of chemical energy—we sometimes say that a person exercising to lose weight is "burning off" excess body fat. Photosynthesis (see pages 22–23) involves chemical energy.

Chemical energy is changed to electrical energy in batteries—portable supplies of electricity. There are various types, but they all work in the same way: different chemicals react together gradually to produce an electric current (see pages 38–39).

5. When the eruption has died down, stir the contents of the volcano bottle with the long stick and add more colored solution for a repeat performance.

FOOD AS FUEL

Food is the fuel that supplies humans and animals with energy. We use energy all the time. Even when we are sleeping, our bodies are using the energy extracted from the food we have eaten to keep our heart, lungs, and other body organs working.

Humans and animals get their energy from plant or animal foods, or a mixture of the two. Plants are the starting point of food chains: they take the sun's energy to produce food in their leaves (see pages 22–23).

Potatoes, bread, and bananas are some of the foods that are naturally rich in carbohydrates, our main source of energy. Carbohydrates are found in starchy foods.

Plants may in turn be eaten by animals that depend on plants for food to get their energy. Those animals may be eaten by other animals or humans. Each new consumer extracts its energy from the previous link in the food chain.

We need a variety of foods for different purposes, but the main energy foods are carbohydrates.

These children are burning up a lot of energy as they play. If you always eat more food than you burn up each day, then you are likely to accumulate fat.

Carbohydrates are found in sugars of various types and in starchy foods such as potatoes, bread, and pasta. The chemical energy in these foods, which is measured in kilojoules (kJ), is stored as body fat. When we need to call on our energy reserves, our bodies convert the chemical energy in the body fat into the kinetic energy of moving muscles.

Different people require different amounts of energy foods. An office worker, for example, needs a lot less than a construction worker or a weightlifter. People who regularly eat more than they need will gradually accumulate fat.

MONITOR YOUR ENERGY INTAKE

MATERIALS
- kitchen scales
- a notebook and pencil
- a calculator
- a diet book

1. As you go through a day, make a list of all the things you eat and their amounts. Loose items, like breakfast cereals, should be measured on the scales.

2. Using the information on the food packaging, the chart below, or a diet book, count your energy intake in kilojoules (kJ) over a day.

Food	Energy (kJ)
Bacon (1 slice)	200
Egg	330
Potato (1 medium)	400
Bread and butter (1 slice)	500
Sugar (1 teaspoonful)	75
Milk (whole, 8-oz. [227 ml])	660
Banana	475
Cookie (1)	400

3. Repeat the project on two or three days. What is your average daily intake in kJ? The "right" intake will vary from person to person. For 12-year-olds, it's about 9,000 to 11,000 kJ for boys, and about 9,000 to 10,500 for girls, but a lot will depend on your build and how active you are.

FUEL SOURCES

The main fossil fuels are oil, coal, and natural gas. They are called "fossil" fuels because they formed from the remains of plants and animals millions of years ago. Those plants obtained their energy from the sun, so when we use fossil fuels we can picture ourselves using "fossilized sunlight."

In the Western world, we obtain most of our energy from fossil fuels. Coal is no longer widely used to heat our homes directly, but both coal and oil are used to generate electricity in power plants. Natural gas is used for heating and cooking. The gasoline and diesel we use for our cars and trucks and aviation fuel all come from oil.

New deposits of coal and oil are still being found, but we are using up these fuels very quickly. Someday they

An offshore oil drilling platform in the North Sea

could be used up completely. We cannot wait millions of years for more coal and oil to form. Because these fossil fuels cannot be renewed they are known as "nonrenewable" energy sources. Fossil fuels also cause a great deal of pollution when they are burned.

Other sources of energy are called "renewable" because they can be renewed: however much we use, there is always more "on tap." Renewable energy includes solar energy and energy from winds, rivers, and tides. The amount of energy captured in one day by a windmill, for example, will not affect the strength of the wind the following day. Furthermore, using renewable energy does not pollute the atmosphere.

In the last fifty years, nuclear energy has been used to make electricity. But nuclear energy has turned out to be less attractive than it first seemed. Nuclear power plants are expensive to build and can pose a serious threat to life if something goes wrong. The waste products produced in nuclear power plants are highly radioactive and have to be stored very carefully for long periods— hundreds of years in some cases— before they stop being harmful.

The Diablo Canyon nuclear power plant in California. Beneath the white domes are the plant's two reactors.

WHAT FUELS ARE USED IN YOUR HOME?

MATERIALS
• a notebook and pencil

1. Find out what fuels are used where you live. Think about how to do this. An obvious way is to list all things that use electricity, all things that use gas, and so on.

2. Make one list for fuel used inside the house. Does the stove run on electricity or gas? Is the heating in your home fired by gas or oil? Make a second list for fuel used outside the house. For example, does your family's car run on gasoline or diesel fuel?

3. Find out how much your family spends on different types of fuel in one year. Ask your parents to show you heating bills for your household to find this out. Does the fuel use vary at different times of year?

4. How much use is made of renewable energy sources where you live? Would it be possible to change from nonrenewable to renewable energy, even for some small things?

5. Ask some friends to do their own surveys, and compare your findings. Can you think of a way to combine everyone's results?

WIND AND AIR

Like nearly all forms of energy, wind energy can be traced back to the sun. When warm air rises from land warmed by the sun, cold air flows in to take its place. This flow of air is a wind. The process will continue as long as the sun keeps shining, so wind is a renewable energy source.

Problems with fossil fuels (pages 30–31) have led to an interest in harnessing wind energy and converting it to electrical energy. The windmills built for this purpose are called wind turbines, and look very different from the traditional windmills of Holland. Generating electricity in this way also has its problems: winds don't blow steadily, and they don't blow all the time. And some wind turbines are large and noisy.

Air can provide us with energy in other ways. Energy from other sources can be stored by using it to "squeeze" air (or other gases) so that the air takes up much less space. This compressed air can be kept in metal cylinders and released to power tools like pneumatic drills and paint sprayers. Aerosol cans also work by releasing a compressed gas that comes out as a spray.

A windfarm is made up of a group of turbines working together to generate electricity by harnessing energy from the wind. This windfarm is in the Mojave Desert in California. Large windfarms have many thousands of turbines.

A BALLOON HOVERCRAFT

1. Mark the center of the square of balsa wood by drawing two straight lines diagonally from corner to corner. Make a $1/16$-in. (1.5 mm) hole through the center.

2. Remove the inner ink tube from the pen. Use the hacksaw to cut a 2.5-in. (6-cm) length of the outer tube at the pointed end. Wash this length thoroughly.

3. Cut off a section of the cork .5 in. (1.3 cm) long. Use a bradawl to make a hole through the center of this section. Enlarge the hole by pushing the pen tube into it, but make sure that it is a tight fit around the pen tube. Remove the pen tube and glue the cork section to the middle of the balsa-wood square over the hole you have made.

4. Push the pen tube about .5 in. (1.3 cm) into the neck of the balloon. Attach it tightly by winding the elastic band around the neck several times. Blow into the tube to inflate the balloon. Pinch the neck of the balloon to keep the air in. Push the tube back into the cork.

5. Place the hovercraft on a smooth surface, such as a tabletop. Let go of the balloon, giving the model a slight push as you do so. What happens? Can you explain why?

MATERIALS

- a sheet of balsa wood 10 in. (25 cm) square, or three narrower strips glued together
- a ballpoint pen
- a small cork
- a balloon
- a medium-sized rubber band
- a ruler
- a pencil
- a modeling knife
- wood glue
- a bradawl
- a hacksaw

WARNING!

- Ask an adult to help you cut the materials for this project.

ENERGY FROM WATER

Energy from water comes from the sun. As the sun warms the earth, water from oceans, rivers, and lakes evaporates and forms clouds. When the clouds pass over land, the water falls as rain. Water falling on high ground has gravitational potential energy. As it drains into streams and rivers, and flows downhill, this potential energy is changed into kinetic energy.

Ancient waterwheels transferred the kinetic energy of flowing water to machinery for grinding grain. In early factories, waterwheels provided mechanical energy to drive machinery for making goods such as cotton. Modern hydroelectric power plants convert the kinetic energy of water into electrical energy.

Plans are being developed to extract energy from the moving waters of the

An aerial view of the massive hydroelectric Hoover Dam on the Colorado River

oceans. In France a tidal power plant has been built across a river estuary. Electricity is generated as the tides cause the water level to rise and fall.

A SIMPLE WATERWHEEL

1. Make a hole through the center of the cork by carefully pushing the crochet hook through it. Now remove the crochet hook.

2. Cut around the base of the plastic bottle with the scissors and from it cut out four blades, as shown in the diagram below.

MATERIALS
- a detergent bottle
- a cork
- scissors
- a craft knife
- a crochet hook
- a length of plastic rain gutter
- modeling clay

WARNING!
- Be careful when using the craft knife.

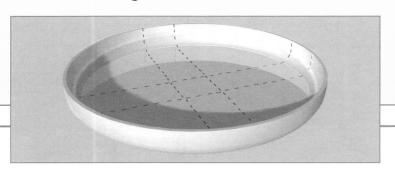

3. Using the craft knife, cut four evenly spaced slits in the sides of the cork. The slits should be just long enough for the blades to fit into, and not too deep. Insert the blades into the cork to make the waterwheel as shown in this diagram.

4. Now make two holes on opposite sides of the bottle, about .5 in. (1.3 cm) from the open end. The holes should be large enough for the crochet hook to pass through freely.

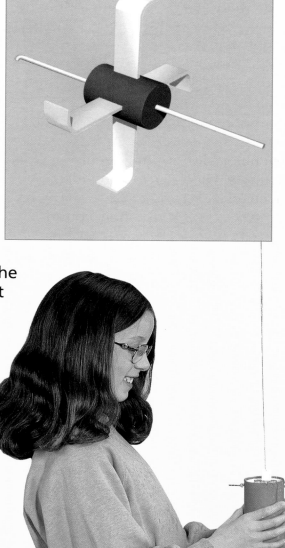

5. Poke the crochet hook through one hole, then through the hole in the cork, then through the other hole. Stick a lump of modeling clay at each end of the hook. This completes the waterwheel assembly.

6. Hold the bottle under a stream of water so that the water strikes the blades to one side of the cork. This arrangement, with water driving the wheel from above, is called an overshot waterwheel.

7. Do the next step in a bathroom. Hold the plastic gutter in the tub with one end of it under the faucet and the other end slightly lower.

8. Turn on the faucet so that there is a steady stream of water flowing. Hold the bottle right side up and lower the blades into the stream. This arrangement, with water driving the wheel from below, is called an undershot waterwheel.

9. What are the energy changes in each case?

ENERGY FROM STEAM

When water reaches the boiling point, it turns into steam. This is called a change of state: the water changes from one state, a liquid, to another state, a gas. Steam is different from liquid water in an important way: besides being hot and containing heat energy, it takes up a lot more space. You can fill a room with steam by boiling a kettle of water.

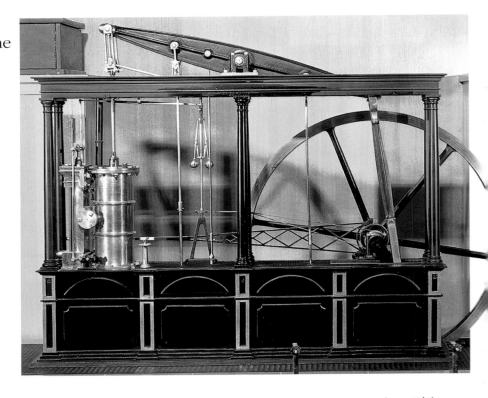

An eighteenth-century steam engine. This steam engine was designed by the Scottish engineer, James Watt, in 1782.

The first steam engines were built in the eighteenth century. They worked by cooling steam rapidly, changing it to a much smaller volume of water. Air would be drawn in to fill up the space, forcing down a piston. More steam would then be let into the chamber, forcing the piston up. In time, different steam engines were developed for driving all sorts of industrial machinery. Steam energy made possible the Industrial Revolution, which began in Great Britain about 1750.

Although railroad locomotives and ships are no longer powered by steam, engines called steam turbines are used to generate electricity. Steam is produced by heating water. The steam is then forced under very high pressure into the turbine, which is a shaft with many blades attached to it. The kinetic energy of the moving steam is transferred to the shaft. The spinning shaft drives a generator to produce the electricity.

> **DID YOU KNOW?**
>
> **The ancient Greeks knew about steam power. In about a.d.100, Hero of Alexandria built small steam-powered toys and novelties. But the scientific and technical knowledge of the time was not advanced enough for large steam engines to be built.**

A STEAM ENGINE

1. Using the hammer and nail, make a small hole about .5 in. (1.3 cm) from the center of the lid.

2. Cut out two strips of cardboard 4 in. x 1 in. (10 cm x 2 cm). Make a hole .5 in. (1.3 cm) from the end of each strip. The holes should be just big enough for the crochet hook to pass through.

3. Tape the strips to opposite sides of the can, with the holes about 1.5 in. (4 cm) above the can.

4. Cut out a vane 2.5 in. (6 cm) across using the foil. Cut slits, and make fold lines, as shown here. Bend each blade up at a right angle.

Fold

Cut

5. Push the crochet hook through the hole in one cardboard strip, through the foil vane, and through the hole in the other strip. Make sure the vane is free to spin on the hook.

6. Fill the can about one-third full with water and replace the lid. Be very careful not to push it on too tightly: it will then act as a safety valve and blow off if the pressure in the can gets too high.

7. Ask an adult to heat the water in the can over low heat. When the water reaches the boiling point, the vane should spin around.

You may have to experiment with different designs of blades to make the vane turn.

MATERIALS
- a small can with a close-fitting lid, such as a coffee can
- a hammer and nail
- a piece of stiff cardboard
- tape
- a crochet hook
- aluminum foil
- modeling clay
- heat source (a Bunsen burner and stand, an electric hotplate, or a camping gas stove)

WARNING!
- Be careful to heat the water very slowly and over low heat.

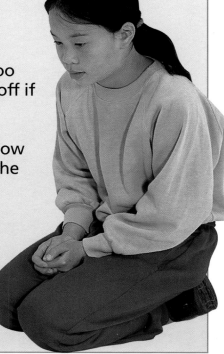

ELECTRICAL ENERGY

Electricity is generated in power plants where steam or water is driven through a turbine, making it spin (see pages 36–37). This, in turn, makes a powerful electromagnet spin inside coils of wire, which makes an electric current flow in the wire. In power plants with steam turbines, the fuel used to produce the steam from water can be coal, oil, natural gas, or even nuclear fuel. Water turbines used in hydroelectric power plants are driven by flowing water (see pages 34–35).

The electricity produced is a form of energy that is very easy to transport over long distances, because it can be carried along cables. This means that energy can be generated where it is convenient to build a power plant, or where a particular fuel is plentiful. It can then be transferred to where it is needed—where industries are needed or where people wish to live.

Electricity is always in the middle of an energy chain. When it gets to where it is needed, it is converted into whatever form of energy is required: the kinetic energy of machines, for example, or heat, light, or sound for domestic comforts or entertainment.

The Eurostar train runs between France and England. An electric train gets power from overhead wires or from a third rail.

HOMEMADE BATTERIES

Batteries make use of chemical reactions between different substances (see pages 26–27) to make electricity. The homemade batteries below use strips of different materials.

1. Wind the middle 20 in. (50 cm) of wire around the broom handle to make a coil. Slide the coil off the broom handle. When the compass is placed inside the coil, it will act as a meter to indicate whether a current is flowing through the wire.

2. Join each end of the wire to a crocodile clip.

3. Fill the container about two-thirds full with water. Stir in salt until no more will dissolve.

4. Connect one crocodile clip to the carbon strip and the other to the copper strip. Immerse the two strips in the salt solution, making sure they don't touch. What happens to your meter?

5. Try changing the copper strip for a zinc strip. Does the meter react differently? What happens if you use a brass strip?

6. Put the salt solution aside, and wipe the copper and zinc strips dry.

7. Push the two strips into opposite ends of a lemon. What happens to the meter? What happens when you try different fruits or vegetables?

MATERIALS
- one carbon (graphite) strip
- strips of different materials including copper and zinc, lead, brass, and tin
- about 3 ft. (1 m) of thin, plastic-coated wire with the ends stripped
- a broom handle
- a small compass
- two crocodile clips
- a small measuring cup or other container
- salt
- a lemon

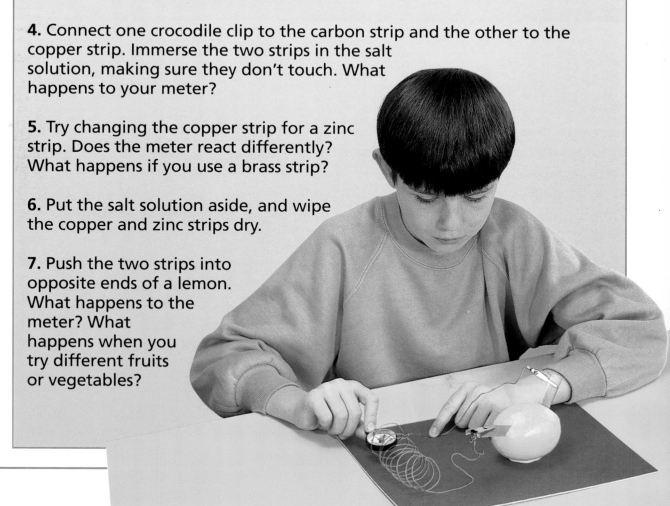

SOLAR ENERGY

Giant solar dishes are used to capture the sun's radiant energy.

As we have already seen, most of the energy we use comes from the sun's light and heat, which reach us in the form of electromagnetic radiation. Infrared energy from the sun heats up the earth in the daytime, and most of it is radiated away into space at night. On average, every square yard of the earth's surface receives enough energy every second to power a small electric heater.

Solar energy, which is renewable energy, can be captured and put to use. The simplest way to do this is to use solar panels, in which water passes through series of black tubes covered with a sheet of glass. The water is heated by the sun and passes into a storage tank. Solar heating provides domestic hot water in many warm countries and is used for warming outdoor swimming pools in temperate countries.

Solar furnaces concentrate heat much more strongly. They generate electricity by using giant mirrors to focus infrared radiation from the sun onto a boiler containing water. The water turns to steam, which drives a turbine. Solar cells, called photovoltaic cells, or photocells, convert light directly into electricity. They are made of two layers of special materials called semiconductors. When light falls on the cell, an electric current is set up between the two layers. Photocells are used to power small items such as calculators and electronic watches.

SIMPLE SOLAR PANELS

Like real solar panels, this test requires a warm, sunny day.

1. Paint the inside of one large container and one small one with black paint. Put them aside to dry.

2. Choose a sunny place to carry out the test. To make the test a fair one, the four containers should experience the same conditions. This means that they should all be sitting on the same type of surface and that none of them should be in shadow at any time.

3. Measure and pour about 5 oz. (150 ml) of water into each container. Cover each container carefully with plastic wrap. The four different containers represent four different designs of solar panels.

4. After about an hour remove the plastic wrap and measure the temperature of the water in each container. You may find that you have to leave them longer than an hour if the day isn't particularly warm.

5. What do your results tell you about the four designs?

6. Think of other designs for panels you could make and test.

MATERIALS
- two large foil food containers
- two small foil food containers
- black waterproof paint
- a measuring cup
- plastic wrap
- a thermometer

DID YOU KNOW?

Artificial satellites in orbit around the earth get the electrical energy needed for their control and communications systems from large numbers of photocells mounted on their panels.

BIOLOGICAL ENERGY

We have seen how food supplies us with energy, and how we get energy, in the form of fossil fuels, from plants and animals that lived long ago. But there are other ways to obtain "biological energy."

When plants or animals die, they start to decay. Tiny organisms start to break down their remains, giving off carbon dioxide gas and heat. Gardeners know that compost piles of rotting plant matter heat up. The warmth often provides a welcome home for worms and hibernating animals. Grass snakes, alligators, and a bird called the mallee fowl all lay their eggs in dead leaves. As the leaves rot, the heat they give off helps to incubate the eggs.

Water plants that die and fall to the bottom of a pond give off methane—called "marsh gas"—when they rot. Biogas generators, which are often used in developing countries, are based on a similar principle. Animal waste goes into a special closed container called a digester. The methane given off by the decaying waste is collected and used as a fuel. Another commonly used fuel in developing countries is animal dung that is dried and used for burning, instead of being used as fertilizer, when it could give back its chemical energy to the soil to help crops grow.

This power plant in Suffolk, England, uses poultry litter to generate electricity.

MEASURE BIOLOGICAL ENERGY

This experiment is best carried out with grass cuttings in the summer.

MATERIALS
- a cooler
- a strong plastic bag
- fresh grass cuttings
- a thermometer
- string
- a notebook and pencil

1. Fill the bag with grass cuttings, and tie the neck with string.

2. Place the bag in the cooler, and close the lid.

3. The next day, measure and record the temperature of the air right next to the cooler.

4. Open the cooler. Undo the bag, and carefully push the thermometer into the middle of the cuttings. Hold the thermometer there for a minute or two. Remove it, and record the temperature.

5. Re-tie the bag and replace it in the cooler.

6. Repeat steps **3** to **5** each day for a week, recording your findings each day.

7. Look at your recordings taken over the week. How has the temperature changed? You could plot a graph to show how it has varied. The temperature to plot in each case is the difference between the two measurements made each day. What accounts for this difference?

ENERGY EFFICIENCY

The world's supplies of nonrenewable energy will not last forever. We need to find ways of making more efficient use of electrical energy so that we can cut down on the amount of fossil fuels we use to generate it. We must also make better use of renewable energy sources.

A modern house in Arizona, built for energy conservation

Energy efficiency in buildings has improved. A major step has been to increase insulation so that less heat is used. A good insulator stops the unwanted transfer of heat and is the opposite of a good conductor of heat. Attics can be lined with an insulator such as fiberglass to stop heat loss through the roof space. Hot water pipes can be "lagged" (wrapped) in similar material. Double-glazed windows have two panes of glass, and the air between the two panes acts as an insulator.

Some appliances have been designed to use less energy. Low-wattage lightbulbs may use up to ten times less electricity than traditional lightbulbs. Modern cars often have engines that travel farther per gallon of fuel than the engines of twenty years ago.

AN ENERGY EFFICIENCY SURVEY

MATERIALS
- a notebook and pencil

1. Look around your home for examples of efficient energy use. Make separate lists for different rooms. You could also note down any inefficient uses of energy you find.

2. Ask about parts of the building that you can't see. Try to find out, for example, if the walls are cavity walls and if they are insulated.

3. Ask a group of friends to do the same survey and compare your results.

Efficient uses of energy

Kitchen	Bedroom	Bathroom
Energy-efficient dishwasher	Double-glazing	Lagged immersion water heater

TEST DIFFERENT INSULATORS

1. Wrap each material around a can and secure with string or tape, whichever is best. Where possible, use similar thicknesses of material.

2. Leave one can unwrapped. This is the "control" against which all the others will be compared.

3. Ask an adult to help you fill each container with the same amount of hot, but not boiling, water. Measure out about 6–7 oz. (200 ml) in each case. Fill the control can too. The water you put in each can must be the same temperature to start with.

4. Take the temperature of the water in each can every minute. Record your results.

5. Continue doing this for as long as the temperature continues to drop by a noticeable amount. Record your results.

6. Think about how you could present your results. One way is to draw a graph of temperature versus time. Is this the best way?

GLOSSARY

Atom The smallest part of a chemical element.

Battery A device that stores chemical energy in a form that can be converted into electrical energy when required.

Biogas A gas, mostly methane, given off by decaying animal and plant matter, which can be used as a fuel.

Carbohydrate A compound in foods that provides energy.

Combustion Burning a fuel to release its chemical energy.

Conduction The way heat energy is transferred through solids.

Conservation of energy An important scientific "law" that says that energy cannot be created or destroyed.

Convection A way in which heat energy is transferred through liquids and gases.

Conversion of energy The change of energy from one form into another, for example, the change of potential energy into kinetic energy.

Electromagnetic radiation Waves that travel at the speed of light and transfer energy from one place to another.

Energy chain A series of conversions of energy into different forms, such as the conversion of chemical energy into electricity into heat.

Fossil fuel A type of fuel, such as coal or oil, formed from the remains of plants and animals that lived long ago.

Fuel A substance with a lot of stored chemical energy that can be converted into other forms, such as the kinetic energy of moving vehicles.

Heat A form of energy caused by the motion of atoms and molecules.

Infrared radiation Heat that is radiated as an electromagnetic wave.

Insulator A material that is a very poor conductor of heat. Insulators are used to stop heat energy from escaping.

Kilojoule A commonly used unit of energy. Also written as kJ. (One kJ is about 4 calories.)

Kinetic energy The energy of a moving object.

Molecule The smallest part of a chemical compound.

Photosynthesis How plants convert the energy in sunlight to chemical energy for food.

Photovoltaic cell A device, made with materials called semiconductors, that converts sunlight into electricity.

Potential energy The energy stored in an object.

Radiation A way in which heat energy is transferred through gases, and the only way it can travel through a vacuum.

Renewable energy Energy that comes from a source that does not run out. Wind energy is renewable but energy from oil is nonrenewable.

Solar panel A glass "sandwich" of tubes through which water passes and is heated by the sun's rays.

Transfer of energy The movement of energy from one place to another.

BOOKS TO READ

Challoner, Jack. *Energy* (Eyewitness Science). New York: Dorling Kindersley, 1993.

Friedhoffer, Robert. *Force, Motion, and Energy* (Scientific Magic). Danbury, CT: Franklin Watts, 1992.

Gardner, Robert. *Experimenting with Energy Conservation* (Venture Books). Danbury, CT: Franklin Watts, 1992.

Gutnik, Martin J. & Browne-Gutnik, Natalie. *Projects That Explore Energy* (Investigate!) Brookfield, CT: Millbrook Press, 1994.

Kerrod, Robin. *Force and Motion* (Let's Investigate Science). Tarrytown, NY: Marshall Cavendish, 1993.

Sauvain, Philip. *Motion* (Way It Works). Parsippany, NJ: Silver Burdett Press, 1992.

Snedden, Robert. *Energy* (Science Horizons). New York: Chelsea House, 1995.

White, Larry. *Energy: Simple Experiments for Young Scientists* (Gateway Science). Brookfield, CT: Millbrook Press, 1995.

ANSWERS TO QUESTIONS

Answers to questions posed in the projects.

Page 6 Both nuts will swing at first, but then one will almost stop. The other nut will keep swinging, but soon it will nearly stop and the first nut will start to swing again. This "cycle" will continue, as energy is transferred through the string from one weight to the other.

Page 7 (1) When two ball bearings together strike the stationary chain of ball bearings, their kinetic energy is transferred through the chain and the two at the other end move off. (2) A small water wave will spread out in the form of circular "ripples." The cork will bob up and down, but it won't move toward the edge of the bowl.

Pages 8–9 The higher the starting line on the ramp, the more potential energy the car will have, the more kinetic energy it will gain as it goes down the slope, and the farther it will travel. A heavier car would gain more kinetic energy, but it wouldn't go any faster.

Page 11 (1) Noise and heat are usually the most common unwanted forms of energy at the end of energy chains. (2) As the circle gets smaller, the container will complete more "orbits" in the same amount of time. Because it still has the same amount of kinetic energy, and its mass isn't changing, it needs to travel the same distance in a particular time. The circumference of the smaller circle is less than that of the large circle, so the container orbits more quickly in the smaller circle.

Pages 12–13 The more twists of the band, the more energy is stored in the crawler, and the farther it will travel. A thicker band will store more energy when twisted than a thinner one. When the crawler goes up a ramp, some of the band's energy is converted into potential energy, and less into kinetic energy, so it travels a shorter distance forward than it would on a level surface.

Page 13 (2) The can rolls away, and then rolls back again. When the can is gently rolled away, the heavy nut stays hanging below the rubber band, causing the rubber band to twist. The energy thus stored is then released as the rubber band untwists, causing the can to roll back again.

Page 15 As the tubing gets hotter, it will expand. This causes the darning needle to roll along the block a little, turning the gauge.

Page 17 The pin nearest the mug falls first, then the others, in order from the mug. After the first two pins have fallen, you should find that the interval between the "drops" gets longer. That is because the speed at which heat is conducted from one point on the wire to the next depends on the temperature difference between the points. Heat is being radiated away from the wire all the time, so the temperature difference between successive pairs of points gets smaller as you move along the wire. Heat is conducted swiftly along the parts of the wire nearest the mug, and more slowly toward the other end.

Page 33 The air expelled from the balloon creates a "cushion" of air under the balsa-wood square. There is virtually no friction between the square and the surface beneath it, so when the hovercraft is given a slight push it keeps traveling until the balloon is completely deflated.

Page 35 In each case, the potential energy that the water has at its starting position is changed into kinetic energy as it falls on to the blades (overshot wheel) or pushes against them (undershot wheel), and some of this kinetic energy is transferred to the waterwheel.

Page 39 The compass-and-coil meter will register a current flowing from your batteries by a movement of the compass needle. Different fruits and vegetables will give different readings.

Page 41 The water in the containers painted black should heat up more than water in the other containers because a black surface is more efficient at absorbing heat. Depending on the size and shapes of the different containers, you may find that the water in the smaller ones gets hotter. That is because the ratio of the surface area of the container to the volume of water is greater in the smaller containers. That is why water in solar panels is passed through narrow tubes.

Page 43 You should find that the temperature increases as the cuttings begin to rot. You may find that the process takes a day or so to start. It is important to take the temperature of the surroundings each time because, although the container is insulated, the outside temperature will have some effect on the temperature of the cuttings.

INDEX